D1202310

HISTORY'S GREATEST WARRIORS

GLADIATORS

BATTLING IN THE ARENA

Pliny O'Brian

Cavendish
Square
New York

Published in 2015 by Cavendish Square Publishing, LLC
243 5th Avenue, Suite 136, New York, NY 10016

Copyright © 2015 by Cavendish Square Publishing, LLC

First Edition

Library of Congress Cataloging-in-Publication Data

O'Brian, Pliny.
Gladiators : battling in the arena / Pliny O'Brian.
pages cm. — (History's greatest warriors)
Includes index.
ISBN 978-1-50260-121-6 (hardcover) ISBN 978-1-50260-126-1 (ebook)
1. Gladiators. I. Title.

GV35.O37 2015
796.80937—dc23

2014024966

Editor: Amy Hayes
Copy Editor: Cynthia Roby
Art Director: Jeffrey Talbot
Designer: Joseph Macri
Senior Production Manager: Jennifer Ryder-Talbot
Production Editor: David McNamara
Photo Researcher: J8 Media

The photographs in this book are used by permission and through the courtesy of: Cover photo by Nicolas Moulin Photography/Moment/Getty Images; Bridgeman Art Library/Getty Images, 4; UniversalImagesGroup/Getty Images, 6; Bridgeman Art Library/Getty Images, 9; Jastrow/File:Ludus magnus Rome 2006.jpg/Wikimedia Commons, 10; Diliff/File:Colosseum in Rome-April 2007-1- copie 2B.jpg/Wikimedia Commons, 13; Bridgeman Art Library/Getty Images, 15; Bridgeman Art Library/Getty Images, 16; DEA / A. DAGLI ORTI/De Agostini/Getty Images, 19; Bridgeman Art Library/Getty Images, 20; Eric VANDEVILLE/Gamma-Rapho/Getty Images, 25; Print Collector/Hulton Archive/Getty Images, 26; Roger Payne/Bridgeman Art Library/Getty Images, 29; Sergey Krivonogov/File:Quo Vadis?.jpg/Wikimedia Commons, 31; Carole Raddato/File:Detail of Gladiator mosaic, two Eques fighting equipped with lance, sword and the traditional small round shield, Römerhalle, Bad Kreuznach, Germany (8197211680).jpg/Wikimedia Commons, 32; Print Collector/Hulton Archive/Getty Images, 33; Duncan Walker/E+/Getty Images, 34; Hulton Archive/Getty Images, 36; Illustrated London News Ltd/Mary Evans Picture Library, 39; Bridgeman Art Library/Getty Images, 43.

Printed in the United States of America

CONTENTS

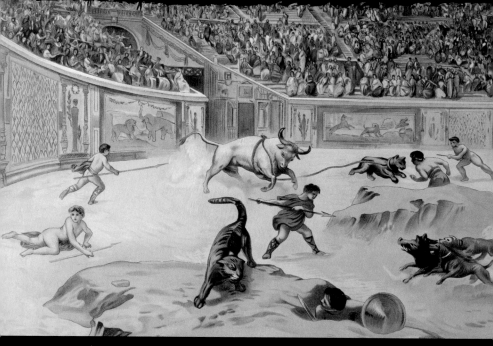

Gladiators fought in a huge arena. Sometimes they fought against wild animals such as tigers, alligators, and wild dogs.

She does not know who or what her challengers are. She has fought against wild animals, trained killers, and unarmed men. She is ready to fight for her life. She has worked morning, noon, and night to ensure she comes out of the **arena** victorious, and alive.

The sun beats down on her helmet. Her wrists and arms sweat underneath her protective leather *manica*. She grips her sword in her right hand, her shield in her left—the weapons that mark her as a *hoplomachus*. She is nervous but confident. Well fed, well rested, and at the peak of health, she is an experienced killer in her prime.

She steps into the **amphitheater** and hears the roar of the crowd. She turns to look at the Roman men pushing and shoving each other to get a closer look. Holding her head high, she waves her sword at the spectators. She will need their sympathy if things do not go her way.

She studies her **opponent**, who grips a **trident** in her hand. Hah, a *retiarius*! She has trained against this type of gladiator and knows how to defeat them. Covered in blood, the opposer whips her net clumsily, clearly a new fighter. Moving quickly, the gladiator avoids the net's grasp. The battle begins, and the two are locked together, fighting for their lives.

Both male and female gladiators would fight to the death for the entertainment of the crowds.

CHAPTER ONE

A DANGEROUS ARENA

"Rome was not built in a day" is a phrase that explains how something truly magnificient takes time to develop. Founded in 753 BCE, few of its original inhabitants could predict that by the fourth century, the **Roman Empire** would be one of the largest civilizations to exist. The city at its heart was the pinnacle of culture, politics, military power, and entertainment.

The favorite form of entertainment for the Romans was the circus, an event that included many different games and races. There were **chariot** races, wild animals such as elephants and rhinoceroses fighting each other, and **mock naval** battles with real ships. The most popular games, however, were the fights between gladiators, the celebrated warriors of Rome.

The Beginning of the Gladiators

According to the Romans, the people of ancient Etruria started gladiator games. Etruria was located in the areas of Tuscany and Umbria in modern-day Italy. Their gladiator fights were held to honor the dead.

The first battle between gladiators in Rome took place in 264 BCE. Brothers Marcus and Decimus Brutus wanted to honor their father, Junius Brutus, at his funeral. Marcus and Decimus ordered that three pairs of slaves, who were also gladiators, should battle each other in front of their guests. These gladiators fought to the death. The guests of Marcus and Decimus were highly entertained by the battles.

Though gladiators first fought at funerals, soon any celebration was an excuse to have them fight to the death.

Gladiator fights soon became Rome's major source of entertainment. In time, these events were no longer held only at funerals, and many events offered the opportunity for **combat**. As these battles between gladiators became more popular, they became larger. By 183 BCE, the games could involve up to sixty battles. In 65 BCE, 320 pairs of gladiators fought in a wooden amphitheater built by Roman general Julius Caesar. In 107 CE, one celebration featured five thousand pairs of gladiators! Games were not just a useful way to entertain the public, however. They also served to show the military power and strength of Rome.

This is the uncovered remains of the Ludus Magnus, the largest ludi in Rome.

Becoming a Gladiator

Gladiators were owned by *lanistae*, who were the trainers of gladiators in ancient Rome. The lanistae ran *ludi*, or special training schools for gladiators, which could be found as frequently as amphitheaters throughout the empire. The largest ludi in Rome was called the *Ludus Magnus*, and was connected to the Colosseum by an underground tunnel.

Lanistae made a living from renting out or selling gladiators. Selling slaves and profiting from them, as a lanistae profited from gladiators, was looked down on in Roman society. Wealthy Romans, however, could own gladiators without shame. In fact, they would hire a lanista to train them.

A lanista rented his gladiators to whomever was hosting a circus or wanted to stage games. Gladiators were also used by politicians to control courts and the outcome of elections. At times, emperors used gladiators as bodyguards, hired killers, or even soldiers in wars. In 69 CE, Emperor Otho used two thousand gladiators to strengthen his army. Marcus Aurelius, another emperor, formed an entire army of gladiators called the Obedient.

TIRO'S TIP

Gladiator battles were called *munera*,
the Latin word for "duties." It refers to
the duty of the living to the dead.

The Ancient Stadium

The ancient Roman amphitheater was
designed to allow a large number of
people to view the games. The creators of
the amphitheater used a circular or oval
design, with bleacher seats. They wanted
the audience to surround the games. In
fact, the word amphitheater is Greek,
meaning "theater with seats on all sides."
Many modern-day stadiums follow this
ancient design.

The amphitheater had some very
unique elements. For example, underneath
the arena where battles took place was a
network of underground passages. The
gladiators waited for their turn to battle in
these underground rooms and hallways.
This is also where animals, such as lions
and bears, were kept. These animals
fought people or other animals.

To prepare for mock battles between ships, the tunnels and passages were flooded with water. The water was then released into the arena so that actual ships could sail and fight each other.

With such a variety of shows, it was very important to have large, well-built amphitheaters. The best example of this type of structure is the Flavian Amphitheater, also known as the Colosseum, located in Rome. It remains today as one of the most prominent buildings in ancient Rome.

The Colosseum has stood the test of time, and still amazes tourists today.

Rome's Colosseum

We don't know who designed the Colosseum, but we have learned a lot about architecture from it. Measuring 160 feet (49 meters) high, the Colosseum was built between 70 and 80 CE, and opened for its first games in 80 CE. Originally, it spread across nearly 6 acres (2.43 hectares) of land and could seat about fifty thousand people. This was roughly a sixth of Rome's population at the time.

About a third of the audience would have been able to enjoy the games in the shade, which was provided by awnings. Seating in the Colosseum was divided by class. The rich had the best seats, while the poor were assigned to the least comfortable.

The Colosseum had eighty entrances to accommodate its fifty thousand visitors.

Gladiators became famous for their battles in the arena.
This gladiator attacks a tiger in the hopes of winning his match.

16

CHAPTER TWO

THE LIFE OF A GLADIATOR

Gladiators had the skill, bravery, and popularity that we admire in professional athletes today. They were some of the superstars of Ancient Rome, and they came from every corner of the Roman Empire. They were people of many races and cultures, and they fought using different weapons and armor. Despite their fame and fans, their glory and diversity, gladiators did not have basic rights. They were not free.

Gladiators were sold to slave owners, and almost all were slaves, criminals, or prisoners of war. Most were forced against their will to become gladiators. However, free citizens could volunteer to become gladiators and give up their freedom for the chance at fame. A new gladiator, or a gladiator-in-training, was known as a *tiro*. A gladiator who fought well and lived through many games was called *primus palus*, which meant "first sword."

Who Were the Gladiators?

There were two types of criminals who could find themselves fighting in a Roman amphitheater. The first were criminals who had committed a **capital crime**, or a crime punishable by death. These criminals did not go to a ludi to become gladiators. Instead, they were forced to fight without weapons, which meant death was certain. The second type were criminals who had not committed a capital crime. These people might enter the ludi to learn gladiator-fighting skills. As punishment for the crimes they committed, they would train and fight for about five years.

Gladiators were often criminals who were forced to fight as their punishment.

Slaves who were strong and would make good fighters could be sold to a lanista for a lot of money. These slaves could earn their freedom if they were able to stay alive for the term of their service as gladiators.

Enemy soldiers captured by Roman armies might also become gladiators. Because these prisoners of war were already trained to fight, they had a good chance of success against other gladiators they would battle in the arena.

Gladiators were sold as slaves. They were often captured soldiers from areas the Romans had conquered.

I Volunteer!

Free citizens who wanted to become gladiators gave up all their rights as Roman citizens and were viewed as slaves. Why would anyone volunteer to become a slave? Some **historians** think that life as a gladiator might have actually been an improvement for many free people. Life in the first century was difficult. The average life expectancy was only twenty-five years. Some people may have thought that taking their chances in the amphitheater wasn't such a bad deal.

Outside the Arena

Although gladiators faced death each time they fought, they were treated well when they weren't fighting. Gladiators lived in **barracks** at the ludi, and were given three meals a day. Doctors were on hand in case anyone got hurt during training or became ill. These benefits were provided to keep the warriors strong for combat.

Regardless of the benefits of housing, food, and medical attention, gladiators were not free. The barracks were like prisons. New gladiators were always guarded and held in shackles. Most gladiators did not like the cruelty of the games. Many even tried to commit suicide.

Gladiators fought about three or four times a year. If they were able to survive for five years, they could earn their freedom. This meant that a gladiator would have to face death, and win, about twenty times. Most never made it.

However, freedom was not the only reason that gladiators fought. They could also earn fame and wealth. Gladiators who survived were paid after each fight. They could also earn a lot of money from their fans and the people who rented them. A gladiator who fought well could even become a hero in the eyes of the Romans. Imagine having thousands of people cheering you while you battle. If you win, they will adore you and scream in excitement. The possibility of this kind of fame even encouraged some emperors to take part in gladiator battles. For example, Emperor Commodus of Rome was said to have fought one thousand duels.

Women Warriors

A large stone uncovered by historians in Halicarnassus, in modern-day Turkey, features a drawing of two women fighters. Their names were Amazonia and Achillea.

It is not clear whether women criminals and slaves were forced to become gladiators, but there is evidence of women volunteers. Historians think that women were as well trained as men and were armed with the same weapons. There are many texts by Romans about women gladiators. The famous Roman historian Juvenal wrote: "Hear her grunt and groan as she works at it, parrying, thrusting; See her neck bent down under the weight of her helmet. Look at the rolls of bandage and tape, so her legs look like tree trunks."

Opportunities for women in the arena did not last, however. In 200 CE, Emperor Septimius Severus banned all women slaves, criminals, and volunteers from competing. Before the ban, becoming a gladiator was appealing to women—so much so that many rich, important women in society were interested in fighting.

The Weapons of a Gladiator

There were a variety of helmets, swords, and shields used by gladiators, and many different ways to fight. Some weapons the gladiators may have used include:

Galea: a helmet with a **visor**, or face protection, attached

Gladius: a gladiator's sword

Hasta: a lance used to spear the opponent

Iaculum: a net used by some gladiators

Manica: armor made of leather that covered a fighter's elbow or wrist

Parma: a round shield

Pilum: a spear used by Roman soldiers and some gladiators

Scutum: a large shield that was longer than it was wide

These weapons meant a gladiator's survival in the arena. Without them, a gladiator would not stand a chance.

These spear tips and swords were once used in deadly combat by gladiators.

A gladiator's fighting style was determined by the armor he wore. The victor in this drawing is the murmillo fighter.

CHAPTER THREE

A WARRIOR IN TRAINING

At the ludi, gladiators kept in peak condition. They exercised and trained in **gymnastics** regularly, and ate a special diet to enhance their abilities.

The ludi was a lot like a school. Gladiators had to follow many strict rules. They took lessons in weaponry from trainers who specialized in different weapons. During training, they used wooden swords instead of metal ones to prevent any serious injuries.

A Variety of Gladiators

There were different types of gladiators in ancient Rome, each specializing in different weapons and tactics. During their training, gladiators could choose the type of weapon and armor they wanted to fight with. This way, the warriors fought with the weapons for which they were best suited. Most of the time, different types of gladiators were matched against each other. The following are some of the most well known types of gladiators.

Retiarius

The retiarius was sometimes called a "netman." Armed with a trident and a net, the retiarius used the net to keep his opponent at a distance. This fighter had to be quick and move around a lot in order to stay safe and win.

Hoplomachus

The hoplomachus gladiator was well armed with a helmet, a round shield, and a complete suit of armor. He carried a short sword or dagger and a spear. The hoplomachus's armor was heavy and slowed the fighter down.

Retiarius gladiators symbolized the god of the sea, and often fought secutors, who represented the god of fire.

Secutor

Armed with a sword and a shield, the secutor wore a helmet and a manica, or an arm guard. The seculator symbolized the Roman god of fire. He usually fought against the retiarius, who represented the god of water.

Thraces

Thraces used a curved dagger and a small, round shield. He also wore a helmet and armor made of leather or metal on his legs. A thraces most often fought the *murmillo* and the hoplomachus.

Murmillo

The murmillo, which means "fisherman," wore a helmet, which had a fish on the crest, and body armor. He also wore a manica. This gladiator carried a shield and short sword for protection.

Dimachaerius

The *dimachaerius* fought with two swords. This gladiator had no shield for protection, so he would confuse his opponent by attacking with many quick blows. He probably wore body armor and a helmet as well.

Gladiators were prisoners of their ludi. Despite being treated well, many hated their lack of freedom.

Provocator

A *provocator* was armed with a shield, a short sword, and body armor. He wore a large helmet with flaps that covered the neck. His chest armor was large and sometimes even covered his shoulders. Unlike other gladiators, the provocator only fought other provocators.

Andabatae

The *andabatae* wore a helmet with a visor, and fought on horseback. During battle, he fought with the visor closed, which hindered his vision.

Samnite

One of the earliest types of gladiators, the *samnite* used a large, oblong shield and a short sword. His helmet had a large plume, or feather. On his left leg, he wore metal or leather armor.

These gladiators resemble the samnites, though the artist seems to have forgotten to include the armor to cover the left leg.

Gladiator fighting styles came from a variety of places the Romans conquered. These essedarri fight in chariots with techniques the Romans learned while invading England.

Essedarri

Based on the fighting style of the ancient people of Britain, the *essedarri* fought while driving chariots.

Laquearii

Appearing late in the history of the Roman games, laquearii used a *laqueus*, or noose, to catch their opponents. The only protective gear laquearii wore was a *galerus*, which was a type of shoulder guard that protected one side of the neck.

Against Wild Animals

One gladiator game was called the *venatio*, meaning "the hunt." Animals such as panthers, bears, wild goats, dogs, elephants, and camels were hunted. Most of these animals did not survive an encounter with an armed human fighter. Historians know that as many as nine thousand animals were killed in some games. Criminals who had committed capital crimes were made to fight wild animals while armed only with long spears. These gladiators, called *bestiarii*, were considered the lowest class of fighters at the games.

To Live or Die

Although gladiators were known for killing their opponents, they did not always battle to the death. Sometimes they were shown mercy. The decision was often left up to either the audience or the editor, who was the host of the games. A gladiator would put his fate in the hands of the audience by laying down his shield and lifting his or her left hand. Then the arena would be filled with calls of "*Habet, hoc habet,*" meaning "He's had it," or "*Mitte,*" meaning

"Let him go!" If they were especially bloodthirsty, the crowd would call out "*Iugula*," which means "Kill him." Then it was time for the editor to decide.

The editor would announce his decision with a hand gesture. If the gladiator should die, the editor would turn his thumb down or thrust his thumb toward his heart. However, if the editor decided to grant the fighter mercy, he might wave a handkerchief or shout, "Dismissed!" For many years historians believed that an editor would turn his thumb up to mean mercy, but this is just a myth.

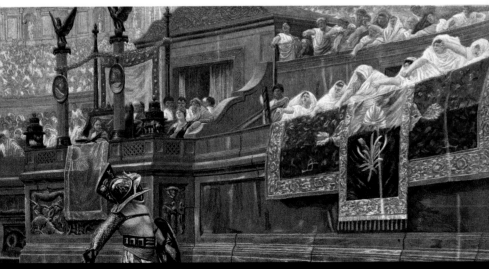

A gladiator would look to the editor to see if he should kill his opponent.

It is estimated that 500,000 gladiators lost their lives at the Colosseum.

CHAPTER FOUR

AN EMPTY AMPHITHEATER

Gladiators and their brutal games lasted for more than five hundred years. The popularity of the games was widespread throughout the Empire. There are many theories about why Roman people enjoyed watching these bloody battles. Some think that watching the battles increased Roman pride and Roman loyalty. Others believe that Romans thought that dying bravely was very important. A few historians have suggested that the games helped keep order in Rome—that having large crowds watch criminals die helped convince citizens of Rome to not commit crimes. The harsh punishment was not only entertainment, but also an important reminder to follow the law.

However, not everyone enjoyed watching the gory gladiator fights. Some philosophers and Christians wanted to end the games. Even emperors disapproved: Augustus Caesar and Marcus Aurelius tried to reduce the number of games held during their reign.

The Legend of Spartacus

Very few names of the once-famous gladiators are remembered, but the legends of some gladiators are still alive today. The feats of Spartacus proved that not all gladiators accepted their so-called fate. Spartacus, a hero to Roman slaves, was one of the most famous gladiators of all time. He is not famous for his battles in the amphitheater, but for his battle for freedom outside of it.

Spartacus was a former soldier, and was not happy being a slave and being

Spartacus was the most revered gladiator of all time. His military background helped him launch a rebellion of gladiators.

forced to fight for the entertainment of the Roman people. In 73 BCE, he led a group of about seventy gladiators to form a small army and flee to Mount Vesuvius, in southern Italy. They defeated many Roman soldiers in battle. However, Spartacus was eventually killed in a battle with Marcus Licinius Crassus, a Roman officer. Thousands of Spartacus's followers were killed. When Spartacus's camp was invaded, the Roman army found about three thousand Roman prisoners who were unharmed.

TIRO'S TIP

Gladiator is a Latin word meaning "sword bearer."

End of an Era

Many factors led to the end of the games. Circuses were becoming very costly to run, at one point costing a third of all the money brought into the Roman Empire. Earthquakes and other natural disasters damaged the Colosseum, which required many expensive repairs. The games also became too bloody—many lives were lost in these violent contests. The rise of the Christian religion also led to the end of the games. Emperor Constantine, who ruled from 323 to 337 CE, **outlawed** the gladiator games in 325, but they continued anyway. Constantine declared **Christianity** the new religion of Rome in 337. Before this, many Christians were being thrown into the arenas because their religious beliefs differed from those of most Romans. After 337 CE, Christians could speak out legally against the games.

One famous legend about how the games came to an end involves Saint Telemachus, a Christian from Asia Minor. During his travels, he visited Rome, where he witnessed a battle between two gladiators. He went into the ring to try to stop these men from killing each other. The audience didn't appreciate Telemachus interrupting their fun. They were so angry that they stoned Telemachus to death. When Emperor Honorius heard of Telemachus's death, he closed down the gladiator schools and declared a true end to all battles between gladiators.

Once the symbol of Roman strength and superiority, the gladiator became an uncomfortable reminder of fallen glory as the Roman Empire began to crumble. Gladiators stopped fighting each other on January 1, 404 CE. By the end of the next century, even fights against wild animals had come to a close. Gladiators were out of a job. The Colosseum was empty. However, the legend of the fierce gladiator has continued throughout the ages. The brutality shown by these warriors still fascinates the world today.

Telemachus attempts to keep two gladiators from killing each other in this lithograph by Dudley C. Tennant. Telemachus's death led to the end of the gladiators.

GLOSSARY

amphitheater A large, open-air building with rows of seats in a high circle that surround an arena.

arena A large area that is used for sports or entertainment.

barracks The buildings where soldiers live.

capital crimes Crimes for which the criminal is punished by death.

chariot A small vehicle pulled by a horse, used in ancient times in battles or for racing.

Christianity The religion based on the life and teachings of Jesus Christ.

combat Fighting between people or armies.

gymnastics Physical exercises that involve difficult and carefully controlled body movements.

historian A person who studies and writes about history.

mock False or imitation, as in "mock battle."

naval Of or related to a navy or warships.

opponent Someone who is against you in a fight, a contest, an election, or a debate.

outlawed To have forbidden something by law.

Roman Empire The system of government that was the strongest in the world from about 27 BCE to 476 CE; the capital was Rome.

trident A type of spear with three prongs.

visor The movable, see-through shield on the front of a helmet that protects the face.

FIND OUT MORE

Books

Chambers, Catherine. *Clash of the Gladiators*. New York, NY: DK Publishing, 2014.

Hanel, Rachel. *Gladiators. Fearsome Fighters*. Mankato, MN: Creative Education, 2008.

Lacey, Minna, and Susanna Davidson. *Gladiators*. Eynsham, UK: Usborne Children's Books, 2006.

Lee, Adrienne. *Gladiators. Legendary Warriors*. North Mankato, MN: Blazers, 2013.

Websites

BBC: Primary History—Romans
www.bbc.co.uk/schools/primaryhistory/
romans/leisure
Find out more about Roman
entertainment, explore animated
timelines, and uncover what really
happened during chariot races.

Classics Technology Center: "Who Were the Gladiators?"
www.ablemedia.com/ctcweb/consortium/
gladiator2.html
Discover the past and present gladiators
of the world through this online resource.

You Wouldn't Want to Be a Roman Gladiator!
www.salariya.com/web_books/gladiator/
index.html
This fun website takes you through the life
of a gladiator.

INDEX

Page numbers in **boldface** are illustrations.